Every Day
with
Jesus®

~

Devotional Collection

THE LORD'S PRAYER

Two Full Months of Daily Readings by
Selwyn Hughes

Broadman & Holman Publishers

Nashville, Tennessee

EVERY DAY WITH JESUS®—THE LORD'S PRAYER
Copyright © 2003 by Selwyn Hughes
All rights reserved

Broadman & Holman Publishers
Nashville, Tennessee
ISBN 0-8054-2735-X

Unless otherwise indicated, all Scriptures are taken from the Holy Bible,
New International Version ® copyright © 1973, 1978, 1984 by International Bible Society.
Used by permission of Zondervan Publishing House. All rights reserved.

Other translations are identified as follows:

KJV
The King James Version

Moffatt
The Bible: A New Translation © 1922, 1924, 1925, 1926, 1935 by Harper & Row
Publishers, Inc. © 1950, 1952, 1953, 1954 by James A. R. Moffatt.

Phillips
Reprinted with permission of Macmillan Publishing Co., Inc., from J. B. Phillips:
The New Testament in Modern English, revised edition, J. B. Phillips 1958, 1960.

RSV
Revised Standard Version of the Bible, copyright © 1946, 1952, 1971, 1973.

TLB
The Living Bible, copyright © Tyndale House Publishers,
Wheaton, Illinois, 1971, used by permission.

Dewey Decimal Classification: 242.64
Subject Heading: DEVOTIONAL LITERATURE/JESUS CHRIST

Printed in the United States of America
1 2 3 4 06 05 04 03

Contents

INTRODUCTION

For many of us, the Lord's Prayer is as common-knowledge as any other passage in Scripture. We know it backwards and forwards, can mouth the words flawlessly even with our minds engaged on something far afield.

Which makes one wonder: Do we perhaps know it too well? Are we perhaps too close to its words and syllables—too close to see that underneath its folds and layers rests a Father's love more complete than we've ever known, a bountiful provision more abundant than we've ever experienced, and a pure glint of God's eternal glory more present-day than we're accustomed to thinking?

Truly, each line bulges with meaning. Each phrase is multiplied into a thousand life experiences. And each time we return to its familiar lines with genuine, open-hearted sincerity, we find ourselves right back in the will of God, restored and renewed, ready to step into life with our priorities in place.

It is our prayer that the Father will make His Son's Prayer come alive for you through these priceless readings. Prepare to enjoy a rare excursion through territory at once well-trodden yet animated with new sights at every turn . . . for a trip through the Lord's Prayer is truly a journey through the entirety of the Christian life.

JESUS' PATTERN OF PRAYER

"This, then, is how you should pray: 'Our Father in heaven, hallowed be your name.'" (6:9)

Today we embark upon an in-depth examination of one of the most precious passages in the whole of the New Testament—the Lord's Prayer. These words of Jesus, so seemingly simple, encompass every conceivable element in prayer and reduce it to a clearly understood pattern.

The Lord's Prayer (or, more correctly, The Disciples' Prayer) is, among other things, a miracle of condensation. In the short compass of 66 words, the Master presents a model of praying that touches on every major aspect of prayer. One writer says of it: "The Lord's Prayer sets the standard for all praying. Everything every man ever needed to understand about prayer is latent in the choice disclosure of these words." That might sound like an astonishing claim, but it is true. No set of theological volumes, no sermon, no series of writings could ever capture the fullness of everything prayer is, as does this simple yet profound model.

The more we understand this model, and the more we pray in line with it, the more powerful and productive our prayer life will become. Because this communication is so important, the enemy seeks to disrupt it. This is why we face the necessity to constantly refocus our thinking on the subject, and seek to deepen and enhance our prowess in the art of prayer. If the Lord's Prayer sets the standard for all praying, then we must lay our praying alongside His pattern in order that our prayers might become more and more like His.

PRAYER

O God, as I begin this quest for a deeper and more effective prayer life, my heart cries out: "Lord, teach me to pray." For I know that when I learn to pray, I learn to live—vitally and victoriously. Amen.

FURTHER STUDY

1 Tim. 2:1-8; 1 Chron. 16:11; Luke 18:1; 1 Thess. 5:17
What was Christ's injunction?
What is Paul's desire?

MORE THAN A RECITATION

*"Don't recite the same prayer over
and over as the heathen do." (6:7, TLB)*

Some Christians think that prayer consists solely of reciting the words of the Lord's Prayer, but, as the great preacher C. H. Spurgeon once said: "To recite the Lord's Prayer and believe that you have then prayed is the height of foolishness." This does not mean, of course, that there is no spiritual value in reciting it, providing we realize that it is not just a prayer to be recited. Personally, I would not want to deprive Christian congregations of the pleasure and joy of reciting together the Lord's Prayer, but I do want to encourage them to view it as a departure point rather than an arrival platform.

If Jesus advised His disciples to avoid "vain repetitions, as the heathen do," would He then immediately follow it by giving us a prayer to simply recite? Obviously, as I have said, one can derive great spiritual pleasure from repeating the words that Jesus gave us, but if we are to obtain the greatest value from the Lord's Prayer, then we must view it as a skeleton on which we have to put flesh. If we view these words, not merely as something to recite, but as an outline from which we must work our way when praying, no matter what we are praying about, then we will experience a growing confidence that we are praying the way Jesus taught.

You see, it's one thing to recite a prayer; it's another thing to know how to pray.

PRAYER

*Heavenly Father, I see there can be great value in reciting
a prayer, but I want to be able to do more than repeat
a prayer—I want to pray. Help me, for without
You I can do nothing. For Jesus' sake. Amen.*

FURTHER STUDY

Gal. 4:1-11; Isa. 29:13; Matt. 23:14, 6:5
What is Paul saying about ritualism?
When does prayer become hypocritical?

SUPPOSE IT HAD BEEN "MY"?

FOR READING AND MEDITATION—
LUKE 11:1-13

"When ye pray, say, Our Father which art in heaven, Hallowed be thy name." (11:2, KJV)

The first word of the Lord's Prayer—"Our"—determines the very nature of the Christian faith. Suppose it had been "My"? That would have changed the whole nature of the Christian religion. Instead of our faith being "our"-centered it would have been "my"-centered—and that would have started us off wrong.

In the field of prayer, as in many other fields, to start wrong is to finish wrong. The word "our" involves a shifting of emphasis from me to the Father, and to my brothers and sisters in the kingdom. It implies a renunciation—a renunciation of myself. We see something similar in the first words of the Beatitudes: "Blessed are the poor in spirit" (the renounced in spirit) "for theirs is the kingdom of heaven" (Matt. 5:3). All the resources of God's kingdom belong to those who are renounced in spirit. So, in the first word of the Lord's Prayer, we find an implied demand that we adopt an attitude of self-surrender—to the Father, and to His interests, and the interests of others in His kingdom. If we do this, then everything opens to us. If not, then everything is closed. The rest of the Lord's Prayer has no meaning and dies if the "Our" is not alive.

Furthermore, this "Our" must stretch beyond our own fellowship, local church, or denomination to include the whole family of God—everywhere. We will never get very far in prayer unless we come to it prepared to sacrifice self-interest, and willing to merge into God's greater plan for the whole.

PRAYER

O Father, cleanse my heart from any limitations I might have in relation to the word "Our." Help me to make it a true "Our" with everybody included—those I like and those I don't like. For Jesus' sake. Amen.

FURTHER STUDY

Luke 18:9-14; Mark 10:35-45; Matt. 23:12
How did Jesus answer James and John?
What was wrong with the Pharisee's prayer?

FAMILY WITHIN A FAMILY

"To all who receive him, to those who believed in his name, he gave the right to become children of God." (1:12)

The second word in our Master's model of prayer is "Father." In Christian circles the term "Father" is probably the most common term used when addressing God, and rightly so, for this is the pattern Jesus set when teaching His disciples the art of effective praying.

This raises the much debated question: Is God a Father to all men and women everywhere, or only to those who are committed members of the Christian church? For many years now liberally minded theologians have taught that God is everyone's Father, so we are all His children, and thus all brothers and sisters. This teaching, known as the universal brotherhood of man, makes conversion unnecessary, and puts to one side the redemptive sufferings of Christ on the cross.

The Bible teaches that God is a Father in two senses. Firstly, He is the Father of the human family by virtue of creation.

12

Malachi 2:10 says: "Have we not all one Father? Did not one God create us?" In Acts 17:29 Paul said: "We are God's offspring." In the sense of creation, yes, God is our Father.

In the sense of a familial relationship, He is not. Jesus said to the Jewish leaders: "You belong to your father, the devil" (John 8:44). Quite clearly, the fatherhood of God is seen in the Bible in two senses. He is the Father of all as their Creator, but He has another family—a family within a family—consisting of those who have committed themselves to Jesus Christ, the Son.

PRAYER

O God, I am so grateful that I know You as my Father— not only in the creative sense, but in the familial sense. May the wonder of this closer relationship grow within me hour by hour and day by day. For Jesus' sake. Amen.

FURTHER STUDY

Rom. 8:1-17; Ps. 68:5; Isa. 64:8
How have we "received the spirit of adoption"?
What is our cry?

GOD IS A FATHER

"I write to you . . . because you have known the Father." (2:13)

We said yesterday that God is a Father in the creative sense and the familial sense. So, for whom was the Lord's Prayer designed—for everyone or only for God's redeemed children? There is no doubt in my mind that it was intended for Christ's true disciples. Obviously many people outside the Christian church find the words of the Lord's Prayer greatly appealing, but much of the appeal is sentimental rather than spiritual.

To understand the Lord's Prayer and apply its principles in the way our Lord intended, one needs to have experienced a genuine conversion. Then, and only then, does its meaning become apparent. Jesus shows us in the first sentence of His prayer pattern that true prayer must begin with a concept of God as Father. Someone has pointed out that the term "Father" answers all the philosophical questions about the nature of God. A father is a person, therefore God is not an impersonal being, aloof from all our troubles and trials. And, above all, a father is predisposed, by reason of his familial relationship, to give careful attention to what his child says.

When we pray, then, to the Father, we must hold in our minds the picture of our eternal Creator as a being who has a father's heart, a father's love and a father's strength. This, then, must be the second note we strike when praying—God is a Father, and we must come to Him with all the trust and frankness of a child. Otherwise it is not a prayer.

PRAYER

O God, I am so grateful that in the word "Father" I discover the greatest truth about You. My heart pillows itself on that glorious and wonderful fact. Thank You—Father. Amen.

FURTHER STUDY

John 5:17-47; 1:12; 2 Cor. 6:17-18; Gal 4:5-6
How did Jesus speak of His Father?
What is God's promise to those who believe?

WHAT'S IN A WORD?

FOR READING AND MEDITATION—
HEBREWS 11:1-6

" Anyone who comes to him must believe that he exists and that he rewards those who earnestly seek him." (11:6)

It is not enough that we address God as "Father," simply saying the word with our lips. We must understand the nature of God's fatherhood, for if we don't, then we will never be able to pray the way Jesus laid down for us. No one can rise higher in their prayer life than their concept of God. If you do not hold in your heart a picture of God as He really is, then your prayers will be short-circuited, and, like electricity when it has nowhere else to go, will run into the earth.

What goes on in your thoughts and feelings when the word "father" is mentioned? Some will have positive thoughts and feelings like warmth, love, and affection; others will experience negative feelings such as remoteness, sternness, or even unconcern. For many people, the word "father" has to be redeemed or amended, because it conjures up memories of unhappy relationships. I believe this is why Jesus, after laying down the structure of prayer in Luke 11, went on to teach us just what God is like, through the parable of the friend who came at midnight. He is not only a Father, said Jesus, but also a Friend.

Christ, knowing that for some the word "father" would have negative connotations, attempted to fill it with a deeper content, by showing that God was a Father and a Friend. We must make sure that our concept of the word "father" is a positive one, for if it isn't, then we will never be able to approach Him with the confidence of a trusting child.

PRAYER

O God, I see that my prayer life rises or falls in relation to my understanding of Your Fatherhood. Give me a vision of Your loving care and concern for me that, in turn, will enable me to come to You in childlike trust and confidence. Amen.

FURTHER STUDY

John 11:5-36; 15:13-15; 14:18; Prov. 18:24
How did Jesus show true friendship?
To what length was this demonstrated?

JESUS REVEALS THE FATHER

FOR READING AND MEDITATION—
JOHN 14:1-14

"Anyone who has seen me has seen the Father." (14:9)

We will never rise higher in our prayer lives than our understanding and concept of God. Time and time again, I have watched Christians struggle over this issue. They ask God for things which in their intellects they know are right and proper, yet fail to get answers to their prayers because, deep down in their hearts, they have a doubt about His willingness to respond to them. Their intensive praying on an intellectual level is cancelled out on an emotional level.

This is why, if we are to learn to pray the Jesus way, we must seek to develop a clear understanding of the fatherhood of God. But how can we gain a picture of God's fatherhood that is true to reality? We do it by focusing upon Jesus.

"The philosophies of India," said one great writer, "are the high watermark of man's search for God. Here the mind of a man strained itself to search for God and speculate about Him. But in all their searching, they never discovered that He was a loving and tender Father. And why? Because they had no Jesus.

18

They had Rama, Krishna, Shankara, Buddha, and many others, but no Jesus."

That lack was the vital lack. For Jesus is the expression of the Father in human form. If you want to know what God is like as a Father, then gaze at Jesus. He drives the mists and misconceptions from around the Deity, and shows us that the heart that throbs at the back of the universe is like His heart—a heart overflowing with unconditional love.

PRAYER

O Lord Jesus, I am so thankful that I no longer need wonder what the Father is like. He is like You. You have revealed Him as He truly is. This gives a clear focus to my praying. I am deeply grateful. Amen.

FURTHER STUDY

John 17; 10:25-42; 5:17; Luke 2:49
How did Jesus show He was of the Father?
What did Jesus pray?

GETTING THE RIGHT FOCUS

FOR READING AND MEDITATION—
ISAIAH 40:25-31

"Lift your eyes and look . . .
Who created all these?" (40:26)

We turn now to focus on the second clause: "who art in heaven." It might seem astonishing that we can spend so much time meditating on one clause of this matchless prayer, but one of the wonders of Scripture is its ability to introduce us to vast themes with a minimum of words. In the Lord's Prayer, a library is compressed into a phrase; a volume squeezed into a single syllable. These inspired words and phrases have become the source of numerous writings and expositions, and none of them, this one included, can fully plumb the depths of all that our Lord was saying.

We now ask ourselves: What was in Jesus' mind when He taught His disciples to pray, "Our Father who art in heaven"? He wanted to teach them (so I believe) the way to achieve a true perspective in prayer. Before we can pray effectively, we must first be convinced of who God is (our Father) and where God is (who art in heaven).

In other words, the initial focus of our praying should not be on ourselves but on God. Doesn't this reveal at once a fatal weakness in our praying? We come into God's presence, and instead of focusing our gaze upon Him, we focus it on our problems and our difficulties, which serve to increase the awareness of our lack. Perhaps this is the reason why, when praying, we frequently end up more depressed or frustrated than when we began. This is perhaps one of the greatest lessons we can learn about prayer—the initial focus must be upon God.

PRAYER

O God, I begin to see now where I have so often gone wrong in this vital matter of prayer. I have begun with myself, instead of beginning with You. Help me to get the right initial focus in my praying. For Jesus' sake. Amen.

FURTHER STUDY

Isa. 40:12-24; Ps. 123:1; John 11:41; 17:1; Acts 7:55
How does Isaiah enlarge our vision of God?
What did Jesus do when He prayed?

"IMAGINEERING"

*"Thou wilt keep him in perfect peace,
whose mind is stayed on thee."* (26:3, KJV)

How many times, when making an approach to God in prayer, have we gone immediately into a series of petitions that have to do with our problems, our difficulties, our circumstances? And so, by focusing our attention on what is troubling us, we end up wondering whether or not God is big enough or strong enough to help us.

In the first six words of the Lord's Prayer, Jesus shows us a better way. He tells us to take a slow, calm, reassuring gaze at God—at His tenderness, His eagerness to give, His unwearying patience and untiring love. The result of this, of course, is that we develop a calmness and tranquility in our spirit which means we will find it no longer necessary to plunge into a panicky flood of words.

In some parts of the world one can enroll in courses called "Imagineering"—courses that are designed to stimulate creative imagination. Most of our problems begin in the imagination—hence the instruction in the words of our text for today. "One can never become proficient in prayer," said one great writer, "until the imagination has been redeemed." He meant that when the imagination is redeemed from self-concentration, sex-concentration, and sin-concentration, and makes God its primary focus, then it becomes creative-conscious, since its attention is concentrated on the Creator and the Re-Creator. And when the imagination is redeemed, all the doors of the personality fly open.

PRAYER

O God, how can I be calm and tranquil when my imagination is more self-centered than God-centered? Help me to be a God-focused person, not only at prayer times, but at all times. Amen.

FURTHER STUDY

1 Cor. 2:1-16; Gen. 6:5; Rom. 1:21; 2 Cor. 10:5 (KJV)
How can we "cast down imaginations"?
What has God given to us?

"God's Postal Address"?

*"He hears me from highest heaven
and sends great victories." (20:6, TLB)*

Jesus, in the opening words of the Lord's Prayer, taught us to focus first on God before presenting to Him our requests and petitions. Why did Jesus bid us pray, "Our Father who art in heaven"? What is so important about the fact that God lives in heaven?

Someone has suggested that heaven is "God's postal address," and, therefore, the place to which all prayers and petitions ought to be directed. I believe, however, that Jesus, in using the words "who art in heaven," sought to focus our minds not so much on God's location, but rather His elevation.

We are so used to living, as we say, "in a man's world," surrounded by limitations, that we are apt to forget that God exists in a realm where there are no shortages or restraints. Here on earth, we stagger from one crisis to another, face endless problems—such as economic recessions, strikes, political unrest—but in heaven, where God lives, such situations are non-existent.

There are no shortages in the factories of His grace, no disputes on His assembly lines and no faults in His communication system. Ring "Calvary" at any hour of the day or night, and you will be put into direct contact with the King of kings!

Can you now see what Jesus means when He bids us focus on God who is in heaven? He is telling us to elevate our spiritual vision until it breaks free of earth's gravitational pull, and to remind ourselves constantly of the fact that, in our Father's presence, our greatest problems turn into possibilities.

PRAYER

O Father, this phrase "who art in heaven" is like a rocket that launches me beyond earth's limitations into a realm where everything is blessedness and light. Help me never lose sight of this fact—today and every day. Amen.

FURTHER STUDY

Rev. 21; Isa. 66:1-2; Matt. 5:34; Rev. 4:2
What is the focal point of heaven?
How does this elevate our vision?

"Settling Down in God"

"I saw the LORD sitting upon a throne,
high and lifted up." (6:1, RSV)

We said that the words "who art in heaven" are intended to help us focus not only on God's location, but also on His elevation. The Savior (so I believe) encourages us, when we come to God in prayer, to get our perspective right, and to look above "the ragged edges of time" to the heights of eternity where God has His royal throne.

The old Welsh preachers and theologians such as Christmas Evans, Daniel Rowlands, and others, used to call this aspect of prayer "settling down in God." They taught that when we gain a right perspective of God and heavenly things, then and only then can we have a right perspective of man and earthly things. It was only when Isaiah saw the Lord "high and lifted up" that he was able to put into focus the events that were happening around him. Our life here on earth can never be abundant until we realize that we have access to resources which are outside the realm of terrestrial things.

A good working translation of the term El-Shaddai (Gen. 17:1) is "God—the Enough." Actually, of course, He is more than enough, but how comforting it is to know that He is at least that. So, when coming to God in prayer, learn to settle yourself down in God. Remind yourself that His resources so infinitely exceed your requirements; His sufficiency so immeasurably surpasses every demand you may make upon it. Get the divine perspective right, and earthly things will fall into their right and proper focus.

PRAYER

My Father, gently and quietly I breathe the strength of Your Almightiness into every portion of my being. I realize that when I see You "high and lifted up," then all of life is reduced to its proper proportions. I am so thankful. Amen.

FURTHER STUDY

Matt. 19:13-26; Eph. 3:20; 2 Cor. 9:8; Phil. 4:19
What was the declaration of Jesus?
How did Paul describe "El-Shaddai"?

TOO CLOSE TO THE GROUND

FOR READING AND MEDITATION—
PSALM 92:1-15

"But you, O LORD, are exalted forever." (92:8)

The reason our personal problems and difficulties seem so large and ominous is due mainly to the fact that we have not brought God into proper focus. When we are able to see Him as He really is—"high and lifted up"—then all our troubles and anxieties are reduced to their proper proportions.

A minister looked through his study window one day into the garden next door. He saw a little boy there, holding in his hand two pieces of wood, each about eighteen inches long. He heard him ask his mother if he could make a weathercock. After getting her permission, he proceeded to nail one piece of wood upright on the low garden wall, then nailed the other piece loosely on top. Soon the loosely nailed piece of wood turned and twisted, first this way and then that, and the little boy danced with delight. He thought he had made a weather-cock that registered the winds, but all it did was register the draughts. "It turned half a circle," said the minister, "when the back door banged."

From where the minister sat in his study, he could see a real weathercock on the church steeple. It was as steady as a rock in the constant winds that blew in from the sea. There are many Christians, however, who are like the little boy's weathercock, always living at the mercy of every gust of circumstance, their thoughts of God fluctuating with their personal experiences. They take their direction from a weathercock that is too close to the ground.

PRAYER

*O God, my Father, forgive me that my life is taken up more with the immediate than the ultimate. I have been glancing at You and gazing at my circumstances. From today it will be different—
I will glance at my circumstances and gaze at You. Amen.*

FURTHER STUDY

Ps. 8:1-9; 1 Cor. 13:12; 2 Cor. 3:18
How did the psalmist focus his gaze on God?
How did Paul describe it?

THE UNIVERSE PROCLAIMS

"The heavens declare the glory of God." (19:1)

We are endeavoring, in line with our Master's directive in the Lord's Prayer, to focus our gaze on the majesty of God. The greater in which God becomes fixed in our gaze, the more realistically we will be able to evaluate the events that go on around us here on earth.

In today's passage the psalmist tells us that one way we can focus on the greatness of God is to consider His handiwork in creation. All around us in this wonderful world, we see evidences of His sublime sufficiency. Consider, for example, the vastness of the universe. Scientists tell us that in relation to the myriads of other celestial bodies in outer space, the planet we inhabit is like a tiny speck of dust in a huge railway station in relation to all the other specks of dust around it, or like a single grain of sand among all the sand on all the seashores of the world. They tell us also that if the earth were to fall out of its orbit and spin away into space, it would create no more disturbance than the dropping of a pea into the Pacific Ocean!

Such word pictures, inadequate as they are, do nevertheless help us form some idea of the greatness and power of our God. Who can meditate on the vastness of the universe without experiencing an expansion in their conception of the majesty of God? Why did God construct the universe on such a grand scale? My conclusion is: He did it to show us that He is gloriously sufficient, unchangingly adequate, and abidingly faithful. How wonderful to contemplate such creative enormity!

PRAYER

God, what a fool I am to think that my resources might run dry. Help me to live in light of the fact that my demand will never exceed Your supply. You are the Enough. Amen.

FURTHER STUDY

Matt. 6:19-34; Luke 12:24; Ps. 45:1-17
How did Jesus focus our attention on God's goodness?
Of whom does the psalmist give us a picture?

"A Time Exposure to God"

"Twice have I heard this: that power belongs to God." (62:11, RSV)

We have seen the futility of presenting our requests to God before pausing to reflect on His unchanging adequacy and sufficiency. We said that one reason why Jesus directed us to use the words "who art in heaven" was to encourage us to focus our gaze on a God who is unaffected by the restrictions and limitations of earth, and who dwells in a place where the resources never run dry. Those who plunge into the areas of petition and intercession before reflecting on the abundant resources that lie in God will find their praying ineffective. They are praying contrary to God's pattern. As the poet says:

> What a frail soul he gave me, and a heart
> Lame, and unlikely for the large events.

However, I wonder if, more often than not, we haven't given *ourselves* "a heart lame, and unlikely for the large events" because we rush into God's presence to present our petitions before taking stock of our spiritual resources.

God offers us infinite resources for the asking and the taking—Himself. The first moments of prayer should, therefore, be contemplative, reflective, meditative. As we gaze upon God and His infinite resources, we take, as someone put it, "a time exposure to God." His adequacy and sufficiency are printed indelibly upon us. No matter, then, what difficulties and problems face us—He is more than a match for them. The vision of His greatness puts the whole of life into its proper perspective. "We kneel, how weak—we rise, how full of power."

PRAYER

*O Father, I am so thankful that Your resources are so near
at hand. I reflect on Your greatness and Your wonder
in the depths of my heart, and my praying takes on
new strength and power. I am so grateful. Amen.*

FURTHER STUDY

Eph. 1; Ps. 5:3; 65:5-7; 1 Chron. 29:12
What was Paul's prayer for the Ephesians?
Ask God to enlarge your vision in this way.

HONORING GOD'S NAME

*"I will do whatever you ask in my name, so that
the Son may bring glory to the Father." (14:13)*

The next clause in Jesus' pattern of prayer is "hallowed be
thy name." What does it mean to hallow the Name of our loving heavenly Father? To hallow something is to reverence it, or
treat it as sacred. It is derived from a very important word in
the Bible—in Greek, *hagiazo*—which means "to venerate, set
apart, to make holy." Does this mean that our veneration of
God makes Him holy? No, for nothing we do can add to or
subtract from His qualities. God is the only Being in the universe who needs nothing and no one to complete Him. To venerate God means to give him the recognition He deserves, to
acknowledge His superiority, and to treat Him with admiration
and respect. So prayer is much more than a way by which we
can talk to God about our problems; it is a vehicle by which
God can increasingly reveal to us who He is.

Some Christians think of prayer merely as a means by which
they can obtain things from God. Prayer, first and foremost, is

a communication system through which God is able to reach deep into our spirits and impress upon us His superiority, His power, and His love.

"I will do whatever you ask in my name," said Jesus. And why? "So that the Son may bring glory to the Father." If prayer does not begin by giving God a prominent place in our hearts and minds, then it is not New Testament praying. Isn't it staggering that the first petition in the Lord's Prayer is not on our own behalf but on His?

PRAYER

O God, help me to build my prayer life according
to the pattern which Jesus gave me, and begin by deepening
the conviction that my first petition should never be for
myself, but for You and Your eternal glory. Amen.

FURTHER STUDY

John 1:1-14; 13:31; 17:4; 1 Pet. 4:11
What was John's testimony of Christ?
What was Jesus' testimony of Himself?

WHAT'S IN A NAME?

FOR READING AND MEDITATION—
EXODUS 34:1-10

*"The LORD . . . announced . . . 'I am Jehovah,
the merciful and gracious God . . . slow to anger
and rich in . . . love.'"* (34:5-7, TLB)

We have seen that the first petition in the Lord's Prayer is not
on our behalf but on God's—"hallowed be thy name." Arthur
W. Pink says in his book, *An Exposition of the Sermon on the
Mount*: "How clearly, then, is the fundamental duty of prayer
set forth. Self, and all its needs, must be given a secondary place,
and the Lord freely accorded the pre-eminence in our thoughts
and supplications. This petition ("hallowed be thy name")
must take the precedence, for the glory of God's great Name is
the ultimate end of all things."

So then, does hallowing the Name of God require us to pro-
nounce it in the quietest and most reverential of tones? Does it
mean that we develop a mystical attitude toward the term
"God"? No. In biblical times names were not just designations,
but definitions. They had varied and special meanings. A name
stood for a person's character, a fact which is demonstrated in

I Samuel 18:30: "David . . . behaved himself more wisely than all Saul's servants; so that his name was very dear and highly esteemed" (Amplified Bible). The people did not esteem the letters of David's name. The statement means that David himself was esteemed.

In the text for today, we are given not just the Name of God, but some of the characteristics that go under that Name. In other words, the Name of God is the composite of all His attributes. When we honor God's Name, we honor Him.

PRAYER

O Father, I begin to see that my object in prayer has been to get the things I thought I needed. Now I realize my greatest need is to give You the pre-eminence You deserve. Help me understand and respond to this deep and important truth. For Jesus' sake. Amen.

FURTHER STUDY

Ps. 111:1-10; 138:2; Lev. 22:2; Isa. 29:23
How does the psalmist link God's Name and acts?
What does "awesome" mean?

"JEHOVAH"—NO SUCH WORD

FOR READING AND MEDITATION—
EXODUS 3:1-15

"God said to Moses, 'I AM WHO I AM.' " (3:14)

We have seen that honoring the Name of God is not just esteeming the letters in His Name, nor speaking His Name in hushed or quiet tones. The ancient Israelites attached such a sacredness to the Name of God that they would not say it aloud. They thought that hallowing God's Name meant hallowing the Name itself. How utterly foolish and absurd! They paid honor to the actual letters of God's Name, yet, on occasions, thought nothing about disobeying His word and denying His truth.

One great Hebrew scholar points out that there is no such word as "Jehovah" in the Hebrew language, although it appears in English translations of the Old Testament. The Name of God in Exodus 3:14, where the Almighty gave His Name to Moses—("I am who I am")—is Yahweh, the English equivalent of which is "Jehovah." The Israelites would not say the word "Yahweh," and eventually the vowels were taken out and mixed with the consonants of another Hebrew word to form the word "Adonai." This was done as a device to avoid having to say the real word "Yahweh." How ridiculous can you get?

Let us be quite clear, then, about what Jesus meant when He taught us to pray "hallowed be thy name." God's Name stands for who He is—His mercy, His compassion, His love, His power, His eternity, and so on. When, as God's children, we come to Him to honor His Name, we do more than enter into a religious routine. We contemplate all that His Name stands for, and reverence Him for who He is.

PRAYER

Father, I see that prayer, true prayer, is not just a technique; it is an art. Help me to learn this art, and to implement what You are teaching me in my prayer life day by day. For Jesus' sake. Amen.

~

FURTHER STUDY

Gen. 15; 22:14; Ex. 15:26; 17:15;
Judg. 6:24; Ps. 23:1; Jer. 23:6; Ezek. 48:35
List some of the names of God.
What do they mean?

PRAYING GOD'S WILL

"Yet not as I will, but as you will." (26:39)

Our first consideration when approaching God is the reverence of His Name. And why His Name? Because His Name stands for who God is. When we reverence His Name, we take into consideration all the ingredients of His character. The phrase "hallowed be thy name" implies that prayer is first and foremost a recognition of God's character and a willingness to submit to it. Jesus put first the determining thing in prayer—God's character. If our petitions are not in line with His character, then, however eloquently or persistently we plead our cause, the answer will be a firm and categorical "No."

I wonder what would happen if we started our personal petitions with these words: "Father, if what I now want to ask You is not in line with Your character, then show me, for I don't want to ask for anything that does not contribute to Your praise and glory." That would cause many of our petitions to die on our lips unuttered. Like the Muslim who washes his feet before going into the mosque, this attitude will wash our mouths, our

40

thoughts, our desires, our motives. We would be saying, in effect: "Your character be revered first, before my desires or my petitions."

This kind of praying puts God's character first and our claims second—putting both in the right place. True prayer, then, begins with God, puts self in a secondary place, and seeks to honor and glorify God's Name. It is characterized by a desire for God's will more than our own will. Any other kind of praying is contrary to Jesus' pattern.

PRAYER

Father, thank You for reminding me that the prayers which get answered are those that are in line with Your character. And what squares with Your character is always in my best interests. I am deeply grateful. Amen.

FURTHER STUDY

Rom. 12; Ex. 32:29; Prov. 23:26; 1 Thess. 2:4

How should we present ourselves to God?

How does this "please" God?

A LITTLE OF ETERNITY

*"And we, who . . . all reflect the Lord's glory,
are being transformed into his likeness . . ." (3:18)*

Why does Jesus insist that our first consideration in prayer
should be the honor of God's Name? Is this a device (as some
have suggested) to appeal to the vanity and egotism of the
Almighty? Can it be that our loving heavenly Father wants us to
give Him what *He* wants (admiration and praise) before He
gives us what *we* want?

No, of course not! God encourages us to focus on Himself
because He knows that in contemplating Him, we complete
ourselves and bring all parts of our personality to health. To
admire, appreciate, respect, and venerate the character of God
is to awaken ourselves to reality. Not to do so is to deprive ourselves and bring about a depletion of spiritual power. We are
designed for the worship and contemplation of God, and
when, therefore, we stand before Him and gaze at His majesty
and glory, the machinery of our inner being whirs into activity,
and our characters take on the features of His character.

God, therefore, has our interests at heart more than His own when He asks us to venerate Him. We "hallow" His Name, and our own name (our character) is hallowed. We gaze at His character, and our own character is made better for the gazing. A shop assistant put it this way: "I just go quiet and empty into His presence, gaze at His glory and loveliness, and give myself time for His disposition to get through to mine."

Yes, that's the secret. Give God a little of your time, and He will give you a little of eternity.

PRAYER

O Father, forgive me for the times I rush into Your presence intent only on getting my needs met. Slow me down and make me a more contemplative person. Then Your character can rub off on mine. In Jesus' Name I pray. Amen.

FURTHER STUDY

2 Pet. 1; Rom. 8:29; Phil. 3:21; 1 John 3:2
How do we become partakers of the divine nature?
List some of these characteristics.

Not Just a "Father"

*"Holy Father, protect them by
the power of your name." (17:11)*

John Calvin said: "That God's name should be hallowed is to say that God should have His own honor of which He is so worthy, so that men should never think or speak of Him without the greatest veneration."

One of the things that saddens me about the contemporary Christian church is the way that some believers refer to the Almighty in terms that drag Him down to a "good buddy" relationship. They refer to the great God of creation as "The Man Upstairs" or "My Partner in the Sky." When people talk about God in such low-level terms, they do Him an injustice. And it's not so much the terms but the image of God that lies *behind* those terms which is the real problem.

We must, of course, strike a balanced note on this issue, for Paul himself teaches us that the Holy Spirit in our hearts prompts us to call God not merely "Father," but "Daddy" (Rom. 8:15). Too much of the "Daddy," however, can lead us,

44

if we are not careful, into sloppy sentimentalism. I believe this is why, after the phrase "Our Father," Jesus introduces us to another aspect of God—hallowed, holy, reverenced be His Name. It is right that we think of God in familiar terms such as "Daddy," but it is right also that we remember that our heavenly Father is a God of majestic holiness and unsullied purity. A.W. Tozer was right when he said, "No religion has been greater than its idea of God." Jesus put it into proper focus when He addressed God, not only as Father, but Holy Father.

PRAYER

My Father and my God, help me gain a healthy and balanced view of Your person, so that while I enjoy the familiarity of Your Fatherhood, I am exceedingly conscious also of Your holiness.
In Jesus' Name. Amen.

FURTHER STUDY

Heb. 12:1-14; Ex. 15:11; 1 Sam. 6:20; Isa. 6:3; Rev. 15:4
Where are we to look?
How do we become holy?

A CLEAR PERSPECTIVE

*"Glorify the LORD with me;
let us exalt his name together."* (34:3)

Hallowing God's Name does not mean having some kind of fetish about pronouncing the word "God" in hushed or reverential tones. It is rather hallowing all that God is, His qualities, character and attributes—all the things embodied in His Name. When the psalmist said: "The heathen shall fear the name of the LORD" (Psalm 102:15), did this mean they feared the letters in the word "Yahweh"? No, they feared the Lord God Himself.

At the risk of over-simplifying the opening clauses of the Lord's Prayer, what Jesus is teaching us is to come before the Father with this attitude: "Our Father, who cares for us with true tenderness, and who has in heaven the supplies to meet our every need; may Your attributes, Your nature, Your character, Your reputation, Your person, Your whole being itself be hallowed." Before we start asking for what we want *from* God, we need to have the right perspective *of* God.

I have just been reading some words of Gregory of Nyssa, who prayed: "May I become through Thy help blameless, just, and holy. May I abstain from every evil, speak the truth, and do justly. May I walk in the straight paths, sing with temperance adorned with incorruption, beautiful through wisdom and prudence. May I meditate upon the things that are above and despise what is earthly, for a man can hallow God's Name in no other way than by reflecting His character and bear witness to the fact that divine power is the cause of his goodness."

PRAYER

Gracious Father, I see that if I am to become effective in prayer, then I must get all my values straight. Thank You for giving me a clear pattern to follow, and for reminding me that when I hallow Your Name, You will hallow mine. Thank You, Father. Amen.

FURTHER STUDY

Ps. 111:1-10; 33:8; 34:9; 86:11
What is the beginning of wisdom?
What does it mean to fear the Lord?

"THY KINGDOM COME"

*"But seek first his kingdom . . . and all
these things will be given to you as well." (6:33)*

We turn now to examine the fourth phrase in the Lord's
Prayer: "thy kingdom come." Jesus, after making clear that the
first consideration in prayer is to focus on God's character, puts
as the next issue the establishing of God's kingdom. Any pattern of praying that does not make the kingdom a priority is
not Christian praying. Our text today tells us: "Seek first his
kingdom and his righteousness, and all these things will be
given to you as well." If you seek something else first, then your
life will be off balance.

A newspaper report tells of a small town in Alaska where all
the electric clocks were showing the wrong time. The fault, it
appears, was in the local power plant. It failed to run with sys-
tematic regularity, and thus all the electric clocks were "out."
When your primary concern is for something other than the
kingdom of God, then everything in your life will be "out," too.
One of the sad things about church history is that the church

has never really been gripped by the vision of the kingdom of
God. There are notable exceptions, of course, but by and large
the church has missed its way in this matter. One theologian
points out that when the church drew up its creeds—the
Apostle's, the Athanasian, the Nicene—it mentioned the kingdom once in all three of them, and then only marginally. The
church will never move into the dimension God has planned for
it until it puts the kingdom where Jesus put it in this prayer—
in a place of primary consideration and primary allegiance.

PRAYER

*Gracious Father, I begin to see that there is something here
that demands my thought and attention, and I don't want to
miss it. Prepare me in mind and spirit for what You want
to teach me in the days ahead. In Jesus' Name. Amen.*

FURTHER STUDY

Luke 9:51-62; Matt. 5:3; John 3:3; Jas. 2:5
What did Jesus teach about the kingdom?
What did Jesus say to His would-be followers?

THE MISSING NOTE

FOR READING AND MEDITATION—
MARK 1:9-28

"Jesus came into Galilee, preaching the gospel of the kingdom of God." (1:14, KJV)

The Christian church down through the ages has taught about the kingdom of God, of course, but it has never put the kingdom where Jesus put it in His prayer, and given it the first consideration and the first allegiance. "Thy kingdom come." Three simple words in both English and Greek, yet they open to us something so vast that one approaches them like a child standing on the seashore with a tiny bucket, wondering how to fit the vast ocean into it! There is no way one can adequately and fully expound these words, but I hope I can whet your appetite, and then you can spend the rest of your life exploring all that is beyond them.

A couple of decades ago the church woke up to the fact that there was a missing note in modern Christianity—the Holy Spirit. Gradually at first, and very tentatively, the church opened itself up to the Person of the Holy Spirit, and now there are comparatively few churches that have not been affected, to some degree at least, by His power and His presence. It seems strange, when we look back, that we could have remained content with a Holy Spirit-less type of Christianity.

The same strange omission has taken place in regard to the kingdom of God. There are signs that the message is being emphasized by certain groups and churches, but we are a long way from giving it the priority God demands. No wonder the church has stumbled from problem to problem when its priorities are lost or only marginally held.

PRAYER

Gracious God, You who are always reaching out after me in love, and awakening me to new awareness and understanding, help me comprehend the truth of Your kingdom. For Jesus' sake. Amen.

FURTHER STUDY

Dan. 2:36-44; Mark 9:1; 1 Cor. 4:20; John 18:36
What was the prophecy of Daniel?
What did Jesus say about His kingdom?

OUR GOD REIGNS

"Jesus said, 'My kingdom is not of this world.'" (18:36)

The kingdom of God was the motif running through everything Jesus taught. However, I pick up many Christian books and magazines today and find that, with one or two exceptions, the kingdom of God is not mentioned. Yet Jesus made it the central note of His preaching and also His praying.

It is time now to ask ourselves: What exactly does Jesus mean when He uses the word "kingdom"? The word for kingdom (*basileia* in the Greek) means "rule" or "reign." The kingdom of God, then, is the rule or reign of God, His sovereignty, for which we are to pray. Jesus spoke of the kingdom as being in the present as well as in the future. In Luke 17:21 he said, "the kingdom of God is within you." Wherever there is a heart that is surrendered to the claims and demands of Jesus Christ, there the kingdom exists. But there is a day coming, says Jesus in Matthew 8:11, when both small and great will sit side by side in the kingdom, and realize that in God's order of things there are no favorites.

The Scripture tells us also that God has a kingdom which is established in the heavens (Heb. 12:22-28), and the phrase we are studying—"Thy kingdom come"—is a petition for God to let that kingdom extend to every area of the universe where His rule is resisted. We are thus introduced to another great purpose of prayer—transporting to all parts of the universe, across the bridge of prayer, the power that overcomes all sin, all rebellion and all evil.

PRAYER

Father, what can I say? When I see that You have given me the privilege of helping You usher in Your kingdom through prayer, my heart is overwhelmed. What confidence You place in Your redeemed children. May we be worthy of it. For Jesus' sake. Amen.

FURTHER STUDY

Ps. 93; 47:8; Ex. 15:18; Mic. 4:7; Rom. 5:17
What does the psalmist conclude?
What is Paul's expectation?

A WORLDVIEW

"The kingdom of the world has become the kingdom of our Lord and of his Christ." (11:15)

Philosophers have said that if we are to live effectively and securely in this world, then we must have a worldview of things—a cosmic framework in which to live, think and work. The Germans call it *Weltanschauung*—the big picture. When we have a cosmic framework, it gives a sense of validity and meaning to all we do. It makes us feel we are a part of a universal purpose. Many modern thinkers believe that the reason there is so much insecurity in the hearts of men and women is because there is a breakdown of this world frame of reference. One writer says: "Modern man is homesick. He is going on a hand-to-mouth existence day by day, and what he does and thinks does not seem to be related to the Whole. This has made life empty and jittery because it is insecure."

The Chinese have a saying: "In a broken nest there are no whole eggs." The nest, the world in which we live and think and work, has been broken up by sin and, therefore, our central unity has gone. This can be seen on a small scale when the home is broken. Nearly all the children in reform schools come from broken homes. Why? The framework in which they have lived has broken down and has left them inwardly disrupted and confused. As a consequence, morals break down.

Can you see now why Jesus taught us to have a worldview of things? With our eyes focused on the kingdom, we know that at the heart of things there is utter security.

PRAYER

O God, I am so grateful that I am not an orphan in this universe. I have a homeland, the kingdom of God. And because nothing can hinder the establishing of that kingdom, I have a peace that nothing can disturb. I am so grateful. Amen.

FURTHER STUDY

Ps. 24:1-10; 2 Chron. 20:6; 1 Tim. 1:17; Rev. 19:6
What picture does the psalmist give us?
What is his exhortation?

A POSITION OF STRENGTH

FOR READING AND MEDITATION—
1 CORINTHIANS 15:12-28

"The end will come, when he hands over the kingdom to God the Father after he has destroyed all dominion." (15:24)

If people are to live securely in this world, then they must cultivate a worldview. They must see the "big picture." Is this why Jesus, when laying down a pattern for prayer, taught His disciples to focus on the "big picture" of the kingdom of God? Whether it is or not, one thing is certain—when we start off in prayer, gripped by the certainty of God's coming kingdom, our prayers are launched from a position of strength.

Just as I was about to begin this page, a sales bulletin came in the post, and on it were the words: "Get the idea—and all else follows." I thought to myself: When the idea is God's idea (the kingdom) then, indeed, all else follows. What if we were to begin our prayers, however, by focusing, not on the kingdom of God, but on the kingdoms of this world? We would receive very little motivation from such an action. Man-made empires come and go. Egypt came and went. Syria came and went.

Babylon came and went. Greece came and went. Historians tell us that at least twenty-one former great civilizations are extinct. Earthly kingdoms go the way of all flesh.

The kingdom of God, however, unlike earthly kingdoms, is destined for success. Call it triumphalism if you like, but the eventual accomplishment of God's kingdom has more reliability about it than tomorrow's dawn. When our minds are permitted to focus on such a tremendous truth, it will not be long before the heart leaps up in confident, believing prayer.

PRAYER

Father, I think I get the idea. When I focus my mind on the glory of Your coming kingdom, then, against such a wonderful backdrop, my prayers take on a new boldness and authority. "Get the idea, then all else follows." Thank You, Father. Amen.

FURTHER STUDY

Ps. 115:1-18; Phil. 2:10; Heb. 1:8; Rev. 11:15

How does the psalmist relate heaven and earth?

How can we help to bring the kingdom of heaven to earth?

ANOTHER KINGDOM

"Now is the time for judgment on this world; now the prince of this world will be driven out." (12:31)

Although we have been focusing our thoughts on the kingdom of God, we must not forget that there exists in the universe another kingdom—the kingdom of Satan. The Bible shows us that in ages past, there was just one kingdom, the kingdom of God, but, through the rebellion of an angel named Lucifer (now known as Satan), another kingdom was established over which the Prince of Darkness rules.

Every person since Adam (with the single exception of Jesus Christ), comes under the dominion of Satan, and is, in fact, classified as a citizen of the devil's kingdom (Eph. 2:1-2). When, through conversion, we become followers of the Lord Jesus Christ, we become citizens of the kingdom of God (Col. 1:13). Once we receive this new citizenship, whether we realize it or not, we are thrust into the front line of the age-long conflict which has existed between God and Satan, and we become participators in the Almighty's plan to bring about Satan's defeat, and to bring the universe once again under the control of God and His kingdom.

Standing as we do on the cutting edge between the kingdom of God and the kingdom of Satan, the Almighty has given us the most powerful weapon in all the armories of heaven. That weapon is prayer. Our citizenship in God's kingdom entitles and enables us to pray: "Thy kingdom come." And when said with sincerity and trust, those words spell out, every time they are spoken, the ultimate triumph of the kingdom of God.

PRAYER

Father, I am utterly amazed when I realize You have not only taken me out of Satan's kingdom, but You are using my prayer, when it is in line with Your pattern, to demolish his kingdom and re-establish Yours. Help me participate with all my might. Amen.

FURTHER STUDY

Eph. 1:17–2:7; 6:1; 2 Cor. 4:4; 11:3
What is Christ's position?
What is our position?

EATING OUR OWN WORDS

"His dominion is an eternal dominion; his kingdom endures from generation to generation." (4:34)

In thinking through the phrase, "Thy kingdom come," we have said that one reason why Jesus taught us to focus on the coming kingdom was in order to help us get our spiritual bearings, and thus be better equipped and fortified when praying for other things. Just as the mariner has to get his bearings from the stars to be able to put into the right earthly port, so we have to get our eternal values straight before we begin to concentrate on temporal things.

Nebuchadnezzar, lifted up by pride, was humbled and ate grass like one of the cattle until he realized that not he but God rules from heaven. Then he was restored to reason and to the throne. I am afraid that we will have to eat many of our words unless we learn that the heavens rule and the kingdom of God has the last word. Oh that we could become so preoccupied with the kingdom of God that it would affect every part of our being, our thinking, our working, and our praying.

Our own causes are valid only as they accord with the eternal cause of God. When I pray, "Thy kingdom come," I am really praying: "Lord, I pray that You will do whatever advances Your kingdom, whatever brings in Your rule and Your reign, even though my own cause might have to be pushed aside." What a prayer! No wonder the ancient Jewish Talmud said that "the prayer in which there is no mention of the kingdom of God is no prayer at all." It's only when we get God's kingdom values straight that we can pray this prayer with assurance.

PRAYER

O Father, help me to pray this prayer, not only with my lips, but with my whole heart. May my life be so geared to Your cause that my own cause may take second place. In Jesus' Name. Amen.

FURTHER STUDY

Mark 4:30-41; Isa. 9:7; Dan. 7:13-14; Luke 1:32-33
Write out your own definition of "the kingdom."
To what did Jesus liken the kingdom?

"THY WILL BE DONE"

*"Praise the LORD, you his angels,
you mighty ones who do his bidding." (103:20)*

The fifth clause in Jesus' pattern of praying is: "Thy will be done, on earth as it is in heaven." If we are to know how God's will is to be done on earth, then we need to know how it is done in heaven. How is the will of the Almighty followed by the celestial beings who inhabit eternity?

First, it is followed unquestioningly. There is no discussion among the angels over any of the Creator's directives. On earth the Lord has to prod to get His servants moving, but this is unnecessary in heaven. *Second, it is done speedily.* Once a command is received, the angels move with the utmost speed to do His bidding. They eagerly wait for the next command so they can hurry to accomplish it. How slow are we, His earthly servants, by comparison. *Third, it is done completely.* The angels carry out His bidding down to the tiniest detail. There are no alternatives, no omissions, no modifications to the divine orders. The will of God is done in full.

A little girl aged seven asked me once, "Does an angel have a will?" I said, "I think so."

"Then how many wills are there in heaven?" she asked. "Oh," I said, "there must be millions."

"Wrong," she said. "There is only one. There were two once, but one got kicked out. Now God's will has full control." I was amazed at such clarity of thought from a seven-year-old. May the day soon dawn when the will of God is done on earth as it is done in heaven—unquestioningly, speedily, and completely.

PRAYER

O God, forgive me for the perfunctory way in which I often respond to Your commands. Help me to be as responsive to Your bidding as the angels of heaven. For Jesus' sake. Amen.

FURTHER STUDY

Isa. 14:12-15; Neh. 9:6; Luke 10:18
Why was Lucifer cast out of heaven?
What phrase occurs five times?

GOD'S TOTALITARIANISM

FOR READING AND MEDITATION—
I CORINTHIANS 15:24-28

"The Son himself will be made subject to him who put everything under him, so that God may be all in all." (15:28)

We continue meditating on the question: How is God's will done in heaven? We have seen that the angels respond to the will of God in unquestioning obedience and perform His bidding with the utmost readiness and willingness. Heaven can, therefore, be described as a totalitarian society.

We are rather afraid of that word here on earth, as it brings to mind oppressive regimes where individualism is discouraged or repressed. I recognize that the word has negative connotations because of this, but, make no mistake about it, heaven is a totalitarian community. Those reading these lines who have had some experience of totalitarianism might say: "What? Are we to emerge from one totalitarian system to become involved in another?" The answer is yes. And God's totalitarianism is more thoroughgoing and absolute than any totalitarian regime on earth.

However, there is a profound difference. When you obey the will of God fully and completely, you find perfect freedom. When you obey other totalitarian systems, you find utter bondage, for they are not in line with the way you were designed to live. However, as the stomach thrives on good wholesome food, and the two are made for each other, and bring health and life, so the will of God and your being are made for each other, and when brought together produce health, life, and fulfillment.

PRAYER

God, drive this truth deep into my spirit, that it is only when I submit to Your reign that I truly realize myself. My will is my ruin; Your will is my release. Help me to lose myself in Your will, for it is only then that I can find myself. Amen.

FURTHER STUDY

Heb. 10:1-12; John 14:31; 15:10; Rom. 5:19
What was Christ's example?
What was His challenge?

"MADE FOR EACH OTHER"

*"I wrote for them the many things of my law,
but they regarded them as something alien." (8:12)*

God demands total obedience; and because this is His will for mankind, then He desires the universe to be a totalitarian regime. It is a regime with a profound difference, however. When we obey completely the will of men, we find nothing but bondage. When we obey completely the will of God, we find nothing but freedom—perfect freedom.

There are many in this universe who think like Ephraim, of whom God complained: "Were I to write for him my laws, he would but think them foreigners' laws" (Moffatt). Ephraim felt that God's laws were foreign sayings or laws—something disruptive. But the will of God and the human will are not alien. They are "made for each other." This expression is inadequate, yet it is the best way I know of explaining the fact that my will functions best when it acts and behaves in accordance with His.

We must take hold of this until it becomes a basic axiom: my will and God's will are not alien. When I find His will, I find my own. I am fulfilled when I make Him my center; I am frustrated when I make myself the center.

And if you are afraid that this depletes you as a person, or makes you into a cipher by subduing your individuality, then your fear is quite groundless. You are really at your best only when you are doing the will of God. Then all parts of your personality are drawn to health, vitality, and fulfillment.

PRAYER

O God, my Father, thank You for reminding me that
Your will and my will were made for each other. When my
will and Yours coincide, then I live. When they clash,
I do not live. Lord, I want to live. Amen.

FURTHER STUDY

Ps. 40:1-8; 143:10; Matt. 12:50; Eph. 6:6
What was the psalmist's request?
What is the testimony of the psalmist?

FORCED TO FACE REALITY

FOR READING AND MEDITATION—
ROMANS 12:1-8

"Offer your bodies as living sacrifices . . .
be transformed by the renewing of your mind." (12:1-2)

Whenever we pray, we are to pray in accordance with God's will. One Greek scholar says that the words "Thy will be done, on earth as it is in heaven" can be paraphrased in this way: "Your will, whatever You wish to happen, let it happen—as in heaven so in earth."

In other words: "God, do what You want." It's not easy to pray this way. If anyone thinks it is, then it is probably because they have never really sounded the true depths of self-interest within their own hearts. It's hard sometimes to pray "Thy will be done" when we know that if God has His way, we will not get our way.

Has this difficulty ever presented itself to you? The basic reason for this conflict is due to the major problem of the human heart—self-centeredness. Paul, when describing a self-centered life and its results in Romans 6:21, ends by asking this question: "Well, what did you gain then by it all? Nothing but what you are now ashamed of!" (Moffatt). The end was zero. That is the inevitable end of a self-centered life—nothing. The major thing that stands in the way of God performing His will in our lives utterly and completely is just that—self-centeredness.

Jesus knew, as we now do, that if we are to become effective in prayer, then we must face up to the question: Whose will comes first—mine or God's? I must be willing to say: "God, do what You want." That is the bottom line in prayer.

PRAYER

Gracious Father, I am grateful for the gentle and loving way
You are putting Your finger on the obstacles in my life.
Give me the attitude that puts Your will first and
my will second. For Jesus' sake. Amen.

FURTHER STUDY

1 John 5:1-15; Jas. 4:13-17; 1 John 2:17
What is the confidence we have?
What ought we to say?

LOUDER THAN "AMEN"

*"I desire to do your will, O my God;
your law is within my heart." (40:8)*

We have seen that to pray the words "Thy will be done" sometimes creates a conflict in us, particularly when we know that God's will is the opposite of what we ourselves want. We must consider whose will is to have precedence—ours or God's.

There are some Christians who pray "Thy will be done," but they do it with an attitude of rebellion and resentment. They believe that they cannot escape the inevitable, and they become angry about it. They say the words "Thy will be done" almost through clenched teeth. Other people say the words with an attitude of passive resignation. They say "Thy will be done," but what they mean is something like this: "Lord, I'm not very happy about the way things are turning out, but I suppose You know best. So I'll go along with it, and I'll try hard to believe it's for the best."

The proper attitude to the will of God, and the goal for which we should aim, is one of rejoicing. It's not easy to arrive

70

at such an attitude, I know, but nevertheless we must have it before us as the desired end.

David, as we see in the passage before us today, prayed this way. If we can cultivate this attitude as our normal and characteristic reaction to everything that happens around us—sorrow, disappointment, disillusionment, frustration, disaster, loss, bereavement—then such a spirit is more than a match for anything. As someone has said: "The Hallelujah of triumph is louder than the Amen of resignation." It is!

PRAYER

God, help me drop my anchor into the depths of Your eternal love, and ride out my storms in the assurance that You are willing my highest good. Help me to accept it joyously. For Jesus' sake. Amen.

FURTHER STUDY

Ps. 100; John 5:30; Eph. 6:6; Heb. 13:21

What is the psalmist's exhortation?

What should be our heart attitude?

"ON" OR "IN"

"The whole creation has been groaning as in the pains of childbirth right up to the present time." (8:22)

In the phrase "Thy will be done, on earth as it is in heaven," what does Jesus mean by the term "on earth"? Theologians have argued for centuries over the preposition used here. Some say it should be "in" earth, and others say it should be "on" earth. I think that the word "on" is the truer translation, but I take the point that some theologians make when they say: "The phrase 'in earth' more nearly expresses the meaning than 'on earth' because God's ultimate will is destined to triumph not only over the minds of men, but over the disharmony and dissolution that is inherent in planet earth."

Paul put his finger on this issue when, speaking by the Holy Spirit in the passage before us today, he said: "The whole creation has been groaning." Yes, and who can doubt it? Despite the beauty of this glorious creation, everything that lives is subject to decay, disease, and death. Life seems strangely poisoned near the fount. The lady who wrote the hymn "All Things

Bright and Beautiful" was only looking at some aspects of creation. She was being selective. She wasn't seeing nature "whole." But Paul did! If you place your ear to the ground (I speak metaphorically, of course), you will hear the groan of a creation that is crying out to be delivered from the effects of sin. But be assured of this: there is a day coming when the will of God will impose itself, not only "on" the earth, but "in" the earth, and will restore this sin-affected planet earth to its original beauty and majesty.

PRAYER

Father, You originally made the earth as You made me: to reflect Your eternal glory. But sin has spoiled both. I take confidence in the fact that one day everything will be restored and Your redemption made known in every part of Your universe. Amen.

FURTHER STUDY

Ps. 8; Gen. 1:26; Matt. 6:26; 12:12
What was God's original purpose?
How did Jesus illustrate this?

DOING HIS WILL—NOW

*"It is God who is at work within you,
giving you the will and the power to
achieve his purpose." (2:13, Phillips)*

We said that theologians are divided about whether the statement of Jesus should be translated "in earth" or "on earth." We decided to examine both prepositions, and today we look at the words "on earth."

Most commentators believe the phrase has reference to the world of human beings who have their home on this earth. In other words—us. Fantastic as it may sound, a day will dawn when this earth will be peopled with those who will do the will of God, not with resentment or resignation, but with rejoicing. That day may not be as far distant as we may think, so we ought to double our efforts in prayer and joyously become involved in bringing our lives in line with His will. One thing is sure—the more you and I conform to His will, the more quickly can His purposes for this earth be realized. John Wesley famously said: "God does nothing redemptively in this world except by prayer." Can you see what he is saying? The purposes of God for the future will have to cross the bridge of prayer.

This raises the question: How committed are you and I to doing the will of God? Are we hindering or are we promoting the interests of His future kingdom? It is vital that we Christians, both individually and corporately, focus our prayers on this issue with fervency and passion, remembering as we do so that the more abandoned we are to the divine will, the more speedily will His purposes come to pass for the world.

PRAYER

O Father, in the light of this challenge today, I feel like praying: "Thy will be done, on earth in me as it is done in heaven." Grant it, I pray, for the honor and glory of Your peerless Name. Amen.

~

FURTHER STUDY

Matt. 3; John 8:29; 1 Thess. 4:1; Heb. 13:16
What was the pronouncement from heaven?
Could this be said of your life?

A CHANGE OF FOCUS

*"I urge, then, first of all, that . . .
thanksgiving be made." (2:1)*

The Lord's Prayer falls naturally into two divisions: the first focusing upon God, and the second focusing on ourselves. The second part of the prayer has to do with our physical, psychological, and spiritual needs. This natural division reinforces the truth we have been discussing: that it is only when God is given His rightful place that we can have the proper perspective towards ourselves.

Jesus begins this part of the prayer by encouraging us to petition God for our physical needs: "Give us this day our daily bread." Some Christians believe that it is inappropriate for most of us who live in the Western hemisphere to use these words, as our problem is not so much where our next meal is coming from, as it is how we are going to have the willpower to keep from eating it! In an overfed, overweight society, they say, our prayer ought to be: "Lord, teach us self-discipline, and prevent us from eating more than we need."

At first glance, the phrase Jesus used does seem somewhat inappropriate, at least for those of us who live in Europe or North America. This prayer might be better uttered by the inhabitants of India, Cambodia, or various countries in Africa. However, to take that view is to misunderstand the deep truth which Jesus wants us to absorb. He invites us to pray, "Give us this day our daily bread," because when we say these words with sincerity, we build a barrier against ingratitude. All that comes from God must be taken not for granted, but with thanks.

PRAYER

Lord Jesus, You whose every statement is filled with light and meaning, unfold to me these words: "Give us this day our daily bread." You have reminded me already that I need to accept Your gifts with gratitude. Help me to be a more grateful person. Amen.

FURTHER STUDY

Luke 17:11-19; Deut. 8:10; Ps. 100:4; Col. 1:12
How did the lepers show ingratitude?
List some things for which you can give God thanks.

WE NEED TO TELL HIM

*"Tell God your needs and don't forget
to thank him for his answers." (4:6, TLB)*

One of the reasons Jesus taught us to pray "Give us this day our daily bread" was because He wanted to build in us a barrier against ingratitude.

Do you pray daily for your physical needs? Do you ask God daily for things like food, shelter, and the other physical necessities of life? I must confess that when I asked myself this question before writing this page, I had to admit that I did not. Now I have made a decision to apply myself to this part of the Lord's Prayer with greater sincerity.

Of course some people argue that because Jesus said: "Your Father knows what you need before you ask him" (Matt. 6:8), then it is pointless to inform God of our physical needs because He knows them already. But the central value of prayer is that prayer is not something by which we inform God of our needs and thus influence Him to give things to us. Prayer is designed to influence us; it is we who are in need of this kind of prayer, not God. *Of course* God knows what we are in need of, but He also knows that unless we come face to face daily with the fact that we are creatures of need, then we can soon develop a spirit of independence and withdraw ourselves from close contact with Him.

Prayer, then, is something we need. God may not need to be told, but we need to tell Him. That's the point. And unless we grasp it, we can miss one of the primary purposes of prayer.

PRAYER

O Father, thank You for showing me that prayer is not
begging for boons. It is becoming a boon—to myself. I pray,
not to change Your attitude towards me, but to change my
attitude towards You. Thank You, Father. Amen.

FURTHER STUDY

Matt. 6:19-34; Ps. 37:5; 118:8; 125:1
What should be our attitude to worldly cares?
What should be our first priority?

GIVE THANKS

FOR READING AND MEDITATION—
PSALM 92:1-8

"It is good to praise the LORD." (92:1)

We pray because we have a need to tell God about our circumstances. To understand the truth of this statement, we must ask ourselves: What happens when we neglect to pray for our daily needs and thank God for providing them?

If we are honest about it and examine our lives over a period of time, we will discover a subtle change taking place in our feelings and in our thinking. If we neglect to pray for our needs, we will begin to take the blessings of life for granted, and gradually, without at first realizing it, we will succumb to the senseless notion that we can provide for the necessities of life, and that we are perfectly capable of managing our own affairs without any help from God.

When we think this way, it is not long before pride steps in, and a kind of spiritual blindness settles upon us—a blindness which blocks our vision in relation to God, others, and even ourselves. We need, therefore, to constantly remind ourselves that everything we have comes from His hand, and that at any moment, should He choose to do so, He could turn off the supplies, and we would soon become beggared and bankrupt. The only way, therefore, that we can build a barricade against this awful blight of ingratitude is to pray daily, remembering, as the poet said:

Back of the bread is the snowy flour,
And back of the flour, the mill,
And back of the mill is the field of wheat,
The rain, and the Father's will.

PRAYER

O Father, teach me the art of continual thankfulness,
and help me never to become bored with acknowledging
Your grace and goodness; otherwise life will begin
to disintegrate. Help me, Lord Jesus. Amen.

FURTHER STUDY

1 Kings 17; Ps. 23:5; Isa. 41:10; Mal. 3:10
How did God test Elijah's faith?
How did he respond?

THEY SHALL BE SATISFIED

"In the days of famine they will enjoy plenty." (37:19)

We have seen that Jesus directs us to ask God for our daily bread because we have a need to ask Him. It does us good to ask, for asking increases our awareness of our dependency upon God, and builds a defense against ingratitude.

I find it greatly encouraging that the God of creation, who is infinitely holy and who holds the universe in His hand, cares that my physical needs are met. This implies that God regards our bodies as important. He designed them and is interested in the way they function.

Some Christians regard it as "unspiritual" to pray about the needs of the body, but, as Jesus pointed out, this is really where our personal petitions ought to begin. While Jesus endeavored to get His hearers to keep their values straight by saying that the spiritual was all important—"Seek first his kingdom" (Matt. 6:33)—He nevertheless put the body in its rightful place, as being a matter of great concern. The Father, we are told, guarantees our physical needs if we seek first the kingdom of God.

Most of the promises in the Bible have to do with spiritual truth, but never to the exclusion of the physical. How much spiritual use would we be to our heavenly Father if He didn't meet our basic physical needs? This is why I do not fear the future. In whatever way people might mismanage the resources which God has placed in the earth, I have confidence in the truth of the verse before us today: "In the days of famine they will enjoy plenty."

PRAYER

Father, help me not to get bogged down in wrong attitudes about the physical factors of my life, for they are a part of me. Teach me to live, physically and spiritually, as one. For Jesus' sake. Amen.

FURTHER STUDY

John 6:1-15; Ps. 37:25; Joel 2:24; Luke 6:38
What was the disciples' attitude?
How did Jesus show interest in physical needs?

GOD'S PANTRY

FOR READING AND MEDITATION—
GENESIS 1:29-31

"God said, 'I give you every seed-bearing plant . . .
They will be yours for food.'" (1:29)

Do we thank God daily for His provision for the physical
necessities of our lives? Some might respond by saying: "But we
never eat a meal without saying grace or giving thanks." Ah, but
are you really thankful? Do you look up into your Father's face
at least once every day, acknowledging that He is the source of
everything, and give Him thanks?

The term "bread" is regarded by most Bible teachers as a
broad term for food. Just think for a moment what God has
provided in the way of nourishment for His children. He has
provided food in the grains of wheat, barley, and so on, and—
according to Genesis 43:11 and Numbers 11:5—He has provided nuts, vegetables, melons, and a whole host of other
things. Keep looking in God's pantry and you will find food
plants such as grapes, raisins, olives, and apples. In addition to
these, there are animals which provide food, such as oxen, sheep,
and goats, as well as different kinds of fowl. There are also fish,

and—according to Leviticus 11—even four types of insects for us to . . . enjoy! How thrilling is His bountiful provision. We eat nothing that did not come from the earth, and every element in it is the work of God. Not to recognize this is indeed the height of ingratitude. As the old hymn puts it:

Its streams the whole creation reach,

So plenteous is its store.

Enough for all, enough for each,

Enough forevermore.

PRAYER

Father, something is being burned into my consciousness:
You are a bountiful and magnanimous God. Keep me
awake and alert, day after day, to Your loving concern
for both my physical and spiritual care. Amen.

FURTHER STUDY

Ex. 16; Gen. 9:3; Ps. 104:14; 136:25; Matt. 6:26
What three things did God provide for the children of Israel?
List the things God has provided for you.

PENSIONERS OF PROVIDENCE

FOR READING AND MEDITATION—
JAMES 1:12-18

*"Every good and perfect gift is from above,
coming down from the Father." (1:17)*

The ability of God to meet the physical needs of the human race staggered one scientist. "On this earth," he said, "with its diameter of 7,800 miles—a trifle too large to play with!—God is keeping in His charge some four billion black-haired or light-haired, two-legged vertebrate animals. What a family—yet He feeds them all."

There are many difficulties and problems facing us today in relation to economy, but the issue is not really that the earth cannot provide enough food. If there is a failure, it is one of distribution, not in production. The food is there, but it is not properly apportioned. A prime minister of India, Mrs. Gandhi, said that there are enough resources in India to feed that nation entirely and still export two-thirds of what it produces.

How wrong is it to blame God for the fact that thousands of people die of starvation each year? The fault is not in Him, but in us. God has given us His gracious promise: "As long as the earth endures, seedtime and harvest, cold and heat, summer and winter, day and night will never cease" (Gen. 8:22). As Isaac Watts put it:

> *Thy providence is kind and large,*
> *Both man and beast Thy bounty share;*
> *The whole creation is Thy charge,*
> *But saints are Thy peculiar care.*

Is it not so? Yet how slow are we to pause and reflect that we are, in fact, literally the pensioners of providence!

PRAYER

O Father, when I think of Your bountiful goodness and grace, I find it difficult to express my feelings. I echo the words of the psalmist: "You open your hand and satisfy the desire of every living thing." For that I am eternally grateful. Amen.

FURTHER STUDY

Jas. 5; Ex. 23:25; Ps. 81:16; Isa. 30:23
What does James say about selfish living?
What are we to live in the light of?

OVERPOPULATION—A MYTH

FOR READING AND MEDITATION—
PSALM 33:1-22

*"The eyes of the LORD are on those who fear him,
on those whose hope is in his unfailing love." (33:18)*

A modern writer tells how once he asked an old man how he managed to live alone in a single cottage, miles from anywhere. The old man answered cheerfully that he enjoyed it since, as he explained: "Providence is my next-door neighbor."

Despite what many politicians and scientists tell us, the problems of this earth are not physical but spiritual. It is not overpopulation that requires our attention, but spiritual ignorance. If people came into a knowledge of Jesus Christ as their Lord and Savior, then they would be given the wisdom to use the earth's resources rightly. Murray Norris in his book *The Myth of Overpopulation* says that only fifteen percent of the arable land on the globe is being farmed, and only half of that every year. It goes without saying, of course, that although God supplies the basic necessities, people have to put some effort into harvesting them; our problem is not lack of resources, nor too many people—it is our lack of dependency upon God.

Paul, in I Timothy 4:3, says that God has created all food "to be received with thanksgiving by those who believe and who know the truth." Can you see what this verse is saying? God has provided us an incredible abundance of food so that we might express our thanks to Him.

The rest of the world indulges with little gratitude. Let's make sure that not one day passes without this prayer meaningfully crossing our lips: "Give us this day our daily bread."

PRAYER

O Father, now that I understand the significance of Your words, "Give us this day our daily bread," help me, every time I utter them, to make them not just a recitation, but a realization. For Jesus' sake. Amen.

FURTHER STUDY

Jas. 2; Rom. 12:11; Prov. 13:11; 2 Thess. 3:10
How does James relate faith and works?
What is Paul's exhortation?

OUR BIGGEST PROBLEM

FOR READING AND MEDITATION—
PSALM 51:1-17

*"Create in me a new, clean heart, O God,
filled with clean thoughts . . . Then I will sing
of your forgiveness." (51:10, 14, TLB)*

What is the biggest problem we face? Some would say ill health; others, lack of money; still others, uncertainty about the future, or fear of dying. My own view is that the biggest problem with which human beings have to grapple is the problem of guilt. It is the most powerfully destructive force in the personality. We cannot live with guilt—that is, truly live.

When I was a young Christian, I heard some great preaching in my native Wales, most of which focused on how God was able to release us from the guilt of inbred sin. Nowadays, apart from a few exceptions, that message is hardly heard in the pulpits of the Principality, nor for that matter in many other pulpits. The emphasis ceased to appeal to the modern mind, and so was discarded. However, it is now coming back to us through the science of psychology. Someone said that the point at which psychology and religion meet is at the point of guilt.

Christianity and the social sciences underline what the human heart knows so well: it cannot live comfortably with guilt.

In this simple prayer of Jesus, however, we have an adequate answer: "Forgive us our trespasses, as we forgive those who trespass against us." If we have fully accepted the forgiveness of God, and we know that our sins have been forgiven, then the result is a pervading sense of peace. The human heart cannot be put off by subterfuge; it needs reconciliation, forgiveness, and assurance.

PRAYER

O God, my Father, I see that within the ways of men,
You have a way—a way that is written into the nature
of reality. And that way is the way of forgiveness.
May I ever walk in it. For Jesus' sake. Amen.

FURTHER STUDY

John 8:1-11; Ps. 40:12; 38:4; 73:21
What made the Pharisees leave?
How did Jesus respond to the woman?

GOD'S THORN HEDGES

FOR READING AND MEDITATION—
ROMANS 3:21-31

"In his forbearance he had left the sins
committed beforehand unpunished." (3:25)

There are some psychiatrists who take the attitude that guilt is dangerous to the personality, and so they persuade their clients that there is no basis for their guilt feelings, that conscience and the moral universe are man-made concepts and must be eliminated. There is nothing, they say, to feel guilty about, so, as some put it: "Let bygones be bygones, and wave goodbye to guilt."

It must be acknowledged that some ideas regarding guilt have to be dealt with in that way, for some guilt is false and needlessly torments many sincere people. However, I am not talking here about false guilt. I am talking about real guilt—the guilt that the human heart carries because it has offended a holy God. You cannot get rid of that by waving your hand and saying, "Let bygones be bygones." Nor can you get away from sin by joking about it. Oscar Wilde said, "The only way to get rid of a temptation is to yield to it." But you do not get rid of temptation by yielding to it. It becomes an act, and then a habit, and then part of you.

No, we are hedged in—thorn hedges on either side. The only open door is the mercy of God. And these thorn hedges are His provision, too. They are God's creation enabling us not to live comfortably with evil, for evil is bad for us. God has so arranged the universe that we can only be truly comfortable with that which is good for us. Guilt cannot be banished by subterfuge. Only God can redeem our wickedness.

PRAYER

O God, I know that although men might be able to help me with my false guilt, only You can help me with my real guilt. I bring my guilty heart to You for cleansing, forgiveness and reconciliation. In Jesus' Name. Amen.

FURTHER STUDY

Ps. 32; Acts 2:37; Ezra 9:6; John 16:8
What was the result of guilt?
What did confession produce?

NOTHING HIDDEN

*"There is nothing concealed that will not be disclosed,
or hidden that will not be made known." (12:2)*

Our text today shows us that no one gets away with anything
in this universe. The Moffatt translation puts it thus: "Nothing
is hidden that shall not be revealed, or concealed that shall not
be made known." It will have to be "revealed" voluntarily, and
forgiveness sought, or it will be revealed in us as an inner com-
plex, conflict, or functional disease. But in any case, it will come
to the surface. It will be "revealed."

The young doctor in A.J. Cronin's book *The Citadel* found
his inner problems were revealed. When politics defeated his
proposed health measures in a Welsh mining town, he sold his
standards for money. After his wife's tragic death, he found in
her handbag snapshots of himself taken during his crusading
days. It reminded him of the man he might have been. He knew
his pain was deserved, and he shouted at himself in a drunken
stupor: "You thought you could get away with it. You thought
you were getting away with it. But . . . you weren't."

You cannot get away with guilt, either by waving goodbye to it or by bottling it up within you. It "reveals" itself in your face and in your manner. Lady Macbeth, in Shakespeare's play, said: "What, will these hands ne'er be clean? . . . All the perfumes of Arabia will not sweeten this little hand." Only the blood of Jesus Christ can erase the stain of guilt upon the human heart. When we pray, "Forgive us our sins," we are asking for the reality that God promises to everyone who asks of Him. And the only way we can fail to experience it, is simply not to ask.

PRAYER

O Father, I am so grateful that when I confess my sins,
they are fully and freely forgiven at a stroke. There is no
period of moral probation or parole. I ask—and it is done.
What clemency! Thank You, dear Father. Thank You. Amen.

FURTHER STUDY

Dan. 5; Gen. 3:8; 42:21; Heb. 9:14
Why did Belshazzar call for Daniel?
What was Daniel's pronouncement?

THE DIVINE EXAMPLE

"Jesus said, 'Father, forgive them, for they do not know what they are doing.'" (23:34)

We have been meditating on the need for divine forgiveness, but it is time now to focus on the fact that Jesus adds a condition to this statement. He says that we can only ask God to forgive us our trespasses when we are willing to forgive those who have trespassed against us.

Does this mean that before we can be converted to Christ and have our sins forgiven, we have to search our hearts in order to make sure that we hold no bitterness or resentment against anyone? No. There is nothing in the Scripture that states that a non-Christian receives forgiveness from God on the basis of claiming to forgive everyone else. Jesus is referring here, so I believe, to those who are already His followers. They have been forgiven for their sins, but they now need a principle by which they can deal with guilt that arises, subsequent to conversion, through the violation of some biblical standard. Paul says in Ephesians 1:7: "In him we have redemption through his blood, the forgiveness of sins, in accordance with the riches of God's grade." Grace—that's the basis of our forgiveness when we first come to Christ. But although we have received that forgiveness, we can never enjoy freedom from defilement in our Christian walk unless we are ready to extend the forgiveness God has given us to those who have hurt us.

This is an extremely important issue, for if we fail to forgive those who have offended us, we break the bridge over which God's forgiveness flows into us.

PRAYER

Blessed Lord Jesus, You who hung upon a cross,
tortured in every nerve, yet prayed, "Father, forgive them,"
help me this day to forgive all those who have wronged me in
a lesser way. For Your own dear Name's sake. Amen.

FURTHER STUDY

Luke 17:1-10; Mark 11:25; Col. 3:13; Eph. 4:32
What did Jesus teach on forgiveness?
What was the disciples' response?

FOR THE SAKE OF CHRIST

*"Be kind . . . to one another, forgiving each other,
just as in Christ God forgave you." (4:32)*

We experience divine forgiveness for our sins only as we
extend forgiveness to those who have offended us.

This cuts deep.

Perhaps you might be saying at this moment, "But I can't forgive; I have been hurt too deeply." Then, may I say it very tenderly, but very solemnly, you can never, never be forgiven. "But
if you do not forgive men their sins," says Jesus, "your Father
will not forgive your sins" (Matt. 6:15). In refusing to forgive
others (as we have emphasized before), you break the bridge
over which you yourself must pass.

A man once said to me: "I know I'm a Christian, but someone did such an awful thing to me that I find I can't forgive
him." After spending a good deal of time with him, and getting
nowhere, I said: "If it is really true that you can't forgive this
person, it suggests that you yourself have not been forgiven, and
you may be deluding yourself that you are a Christian." He

looked at me aghast and went white in the face. My counseling methods are not always as abrupt as that; however, this brought him face to face with reality—and it worked. He got down on his knees, right where he was, and said: "Father, because You have forgiven me, I offer Your forgiveness and my forgiveness to my brother who has offended me, and I absolve him of his offense in Jesus' Name." Then what happened? Instantly the joy of the Lord streamed right into the center of his being, and he laughed and laughed, literally for almost an hour.

PRAYER

Lord Jesus, You who forgave those who spat in Your face and nailed You to a cross, help me to open my heart now and forgive all those who have hurt me. I do it in Your strength and power. Thank You, Lord Jesus. Amen.

FURTHER STUDY

Matt. 18:21-35; 5:7; Luke 6:36; Prov. 3:3
How does this parable apply to us?
What is the basis of forgiving others?

GETTING TO THE ROOT

FOR READING AND MEDITATION—
GENESIS 41:46-52

"God has made me forget all my hardship." (41:51, RSV)

Some say, "I can forgive, but I can't forget." But you don't really mean that, do you?

See how this statement from the Lord's Prayer looks when set against that attitude: "Father, forgive me as I forgive others. I forgive that person, but I won't forget what he did. You forgive me the same way. Forgive me, but don't forget my sins, and when I do something wrong, bring up the whole thing again." God cannot, and does not, forgive that way. He blots the offense out of His book of remembrance. So must you.

Perhaps you say: "Well, I'll forgive, but I'll have nothing more to do with that person." Now pray the Lord's Prayer with that in mind. "Father, forgive me as I forgive others. I forgive that person, but from henceforth I'll have nothing more to do with him. You forgive me in the same way. Forgive me, but have nothing more to do with me." You see its absurdity?

Don't try to forget things, don't try to smooth them over, and don't drive them into the subconscious. Get them up and out.

A woman visited her doctor and asked him to give her an ointment to smooth over her abscess. When the doctor refused and said it must be lanced, she left his surgery and went home. In a few days the poison had spread through her system and killed her. Unbelievable? It really happened. The lady was known to me.

I beg you, when facing the issue which is confronting us in this statement from the Lord's Prayer, don't ask for a band-aid or a halfway measure. Get it out. Forgive.

PRAYER

Heavenly Father, albeit gently and tenderly, You are driving me into a corner. I would escape, but You won't let me. Today, therefore, in Your Name, I forgive all who have hurt or injured me. It's done. In Jesus' Name. Amen.

FURTHER STUDY

Gen. 45; Phil 3:13; Heb. 8:12

How did Joseph demonstrate true forgiveness?
How did he see God's purposes in what had happened?

A KNOTTY PROBLEM

"God cannot be tempted by evil,
nor does he tempt anyone." (1:13)

We now examine the third petition in that part of the Lord's Prayer which focuses on ourselves: "Lead us not into temptation, but deliver us from evil."

The first part of the Lord's Prayer relates, as we have seen, to God and His glory. The second part relates to man and his needs. Here, in this third petition relating to our needs, the vital core of human need is touched, as Jesus characteristically puts His finger on the deepest need of the spirit—our deliverance and protection.

An immediate problem, however, presents itself in these words, and it is one over which theologians have debated for centuries. The problem is this: if temptation is necessary to our growth (as we grapple, we grow), are we really expected to pray that God will not do what He must do in order to accomplish His work within us? After all, we are told, Jesus was led by the Spirit into the wilderness to be tempted by the devil.

Over the years I have had more letters about this particular issue than probably any other subject I have addressed. A letter that came to me recently put the problem like this: "If, as I understand it, the word 'temptation' (in Greek, *peirasmos*) means 'a test or a trial,' why should we pray to be kept from it, particularly as James tells us to 'count it all joy when you fall into temptation'?" You see the difficulty, I am sure. There are a number of interesting answers to this question, which we shall look at in the following pages.

PRAYER

Father, as I come up against this problem, which Your people have debated and discussed for centuries, help me, I pray, to come to clear and certain conclusions. For Jesus' sake. Amen.

FURTHER STUDY

Matt. 4:1-11; 2 Cor. 2:11; Eph. 6:13;
1 Pet. 1:5-7; 2 Pet. 2:9

What is the basis of temptation?

How does this become sin?

UNRECOGNIZED TEMPTATION

FOR READING AND MEDITATION—
MATTHEW 26:36-54

*"Watch and pray so that you will not
fall in temptation." (26:41)*

The words of Jesus in the Lord's Prayer include, "Lead us
not into temptation." Why should we ask God to keep us from
something that could work for our good?

One answer to this problem is that Jesus, when using these
words, meant not just temptation but *unrecognized* temptation.
The advocates of this interpretation say that when temptation
is recognized, it can be resisted; and when it is resisted, it then
becomes a source of strength and power in our lives.

One writer, who holds to this interpretation, put it this way:
"If I am filling out my income tax form, and I know that some
income has come to me through other than the usual channels,
and there is no way of anyone checking it, I am confronted with
a temptation to omit it. But I know that doing this is wrong.
No one has to tell me. I know it. And when I resist the temptation, I find I am stronger the next time, when an even larger
amount may be involved."

There is a good deal of merit in this interpretation, for there is no doubt that evil can be more effectively resisted when it is clearly recognized.

Simon Peter is an example of this. Jesus said to him in the garden of Gethsemane: "Watch and pray so that you will not fall into temptation." He did not heed that word, and became involved in a serious act of violence (John 18:10). Peter thought he was doing the right thing, but really his act of violence was due to his inability to recognize what was happening.

PRAYER

Father, this may not be the precise meaning Your Son had in mind when He gave us these words, but I see that it has application to my life. Help me to be alert to every temptation, and give me the insight to discern it and deal with it in Your strength. Amen.

FURTHER STUDY

Gen. 3; 1 Thess. 3:5; 2 Cor. 11:3; 2 Pet. 3:17
Why did Eve succumb to temptation?
What is Paul's warning?

"LORD, HELP ME"

FOR READING AND MEDITATION—
I CORINTHIANS 10:1-13

"God is faithful; he will not let you be tempted beyond what you can bear." (10:13)

One perspective on the phrase "Lead us not into temptation" tells us that, if we pray for the ability to recognize temptation when it comes our way, then we will be able to confront it and turn it to advantage.

Another interpretation explains that this is a prayer for us to be kept back from more temptation than we can cope with. It's like saying: "Lord, help us not to get involved in more temptation than we can handle." This view, as I am sure you can see at once, makes good sense, and could well be what Jesus meant.

One of the biographers of an intrepid missionary tells how, in his early days in China, Hudson Taylor met with several great disappointments. One day, after a spate of troubles, he took hold of a guide who had demanded an outrageous fee from him, and shook him violently. A few hours later, he realized he had denied his Lord by this action, and after searching his heart for the reason why he had succumbed to anger and violence, he realized that he had been so preoccupied with his problems that he had failed to commit his ways to the Lord. His biographer says: "If Hudson Taylor had prayed the prayer, 'Lead us not into temptation,' and committed his ways to the Lord, then perhaps the Spirit would have been able to direct his path so that he would not have faced more temptation than he could bear."

It is an intriguing thought. But is it the fullest meaning of Jesus' words? Possibly—but, as we shall see in the next reading, I think it means much more.

PRAYER

Father, though the meaning of this phrase is not yet clear, one thing is: I need Your help at every stage of my earthly pilgrimage, for I cannot face temptation alone. So stay with me—every day and every hour. For Jesus' sake. Amen.

FURTHER STUDY

Acts 5:1-11; Prov. 1:10; 4:14; Rom. 6:13
Why did Ananias and Sapphira yield to temptation?
What is Paul's antidote?

GOD'S SAFETY VALVE

FOR READING AND MEDITATION—
HEBREWS 2:5-18

*"Because he himself suffered when he was tempted,
he is able to help those who are being tempted." (2:18)*

We now consider a third possible interpretation of "Lead us
not into temptation"—one which I regard as the clearest meaning of our Lord's words. This interpretation was originally
given by Chrysostom, an early church father. He said, "This
particular petition is the most natural appeal of human weakness, and a recognition of our human tendency to stumble on
into folly."

Perhaps, in order to see these words of Chrysostom in a clear
light, we need to set them against our Lord's experience in the
garden of Gethsemane. He prayed, "My Father, if it is possible, may this cup be taken from me" (Matt. 26:39). Jesus knew
that the only way to accomplish redemption for the human race
was by way of the cross. Nevertheless, because He was human
as well as divine, He gave expression to His humanity, even
though, as the writer to the Hebrews said, He endured the cross
for the joy that was set before Him (Heb. 12:2).

You see, even though Jesus knew that the cross had to be experienced in all its horror and torment if men and women were to be redeemed, He still gave expression to His human feelings of dread and apprehension. Jesus did not feel guilty about this demonstration of His humanity; neither was God disappointed by His words: "My Father, if it is possible, may this cup be taken from me." The expression of our human weakness is a necessary part of prayer.

PRAYER

Father, I think I am beginning to see. These words are the safety valve, built into prayer, which enables me to express my weakness and my true feelings. I am so thankful. Amen.

FURTHER STUDY

Phil. 2:1-11; Rom. 8:3; Heb. 4:15; 2 Cor. 12:9
What is revealed through Christ's humanity?
How is this a strength to us?

EMOTIONAL, NOT COGNITIVE

"For we do not have a high priest who is unable to sympathize with our weaknesses." (4:15)

We continue examining "Lead us not into temptation, but deliver us from evil." We have touched on the fact that one explanation of these words might be that Jesus was providing a framework through which we could express our feelings of weakness when faced with the possibility of temptation.

One writer says of these words from the Lord's Prayer, "They can only be properly understood when they are seen, not as cognitive (mental) but emotional." He meant that this statement of Jesus is something that appeals to the heart. It is as if Jesus were saying: "Even though your mind understands that as you face temptation and overcome it, you become stronger in God, there is still a part of you—your emotions—that feels it would rather not face the pressures. I understand this. I have been in that situation myself. So I will provide a prayer framework for you that will enable you to express, not so much your thoughts, but your feelings. It will be an admission of your feelings of weakness, but it will also be a release, for if your fears are not expressed, they will be repressed, and will go 'underground' to cause trouble. So these words will provide you with what you need—an opportunity to give vent to your inner feelings of reluctance at facing temptation."

The more I ponder this, the more grateful I am to God for recognizing that I am not just an intellectual being but an emotional one, and for building into His pattern of prayer a safety valve that lets me express my inner feelings.

PRAYER

O Father, what can I say? You think of everything. I am overwhelmed with the compassion that You show me, even when attempting to bring me to a higher level of prayer. Amen.

FURTHER STUDY

1 Cor. 10:1-13; Luke 22:31-32; Rom. 16:20; Heb. 7:25
What is the way of escape?
How can temptation be turned to good?

ACKNOWLEDGED FEELINGS

FOR READING AND MEDITATION—
PSALM 42:1-11

"Why are you downcast, O my soul?
Why so disturbed within me?" (42:5)

Rationally, I may perceive that temptation does a perfecting work in my personality; yet in my feelings, if I am honest, I would prefer not to face it. Our emotions, as well as our intellect, are taken into consideration by our Lord when laying down for us His pattern of prayer, for He knows that to deny our feelings is to work *against* the personality and not with it.

Psychologists tell us that the denial of feelings is the first step toward a nervous breakdown. Negative feelings must be handled carefully, for if repressed, they are like the Chinese pirates of the past, who used to hide in the hold of a vessel and then rise up when the ship was out on the open sea in order to attempt to capture and possess it. *Then* there was a fight.

One of the most helpful insights I have found in my study of human personality is the fact that we don't have to *act* on our negative feelings, but we do have to *acknowledge* them. If we say with our minds: "Come on, temptation, I'm ready for you," and deny the fact that our emotions feel differently, then this pretense, that the feelings are not there, invites trouble into the personality. When, however, we acknowledge these feelings and admit that they are there, we rob them of their power to hurt us. I see this psychological mechanism wonderfully catered for in the words of Jesus which we are considering. They are the framework in which our feelings can have a vote also. Thus, though not acted upon, they are not denied.

PRAYER

O Father, how can I thank You enough for taking into consideration every part of my personality in this exciting pattern of prayer? I am so thankful. Amen.

FURTHER STUDY

1 Kings 19; Ps. 28:7, 40:17; Isa. 41:10
How was Elijah able to express his feelings?
How did God respond?

EVIL IS BAD FOR US

FOR READING AND MEDITATION—
ROMANS 12:9-21

"Love must be sincere. Hate what is evil;
cling to what is good." (12:9)

In considering the words "Lead us not into temptation, but deliver us from evil," here we concentrate on "deliver us from evil." Notice it is not a prayer for deliverance from this or that type of evil, but from evil itself. To Jesus, evil was evil in whatever form it came—whether in the evil of the flesh or the evil of the disposition, whether in the individual will or in the corporate will. Evil was never good, and good was never evil.

Someone has pointed out that the word "evil" is the word "live" spelled backwards. Evil, then, could be said to be anti-life. Non-Christians are finding out how not to live the hard way. They think they know better than God, and follow a way of their own choosing, only to find, like the rats in the scientific experiments who go down the wrong path, that there are wires at the end which carry electric shocks. These shocks are of various kinds: neuroses, inner conflicts, as well as some forms of physical illness.

Society is concerned about a disease called sexual herpes which is spread through sexual permissiveness. God has made it impossible for us to live against His design or harm ourselves without His protest. And He protests because he loves us.

We can decide to have done with evil. The best way to deal with evil is to keep away from it, hence the prayer "Lead us not into temptation, but deliver us from evil." I say again, evil is bad for us, and good is good for us.

PRAYER

My Father, You who made me for good, because goodness is good for me, help me to abstain, not only from evil, but from the very appearance of it. For Your own dear Name's sake. Amen.

FURTHER STUDY

Gen. 39; 1 Cor. 10:6; 1 Thess. 5:22;
1 Pet. 3:11; 2 Tim. 2:22
How did Joseph resist temptation?
What did Paul advise Timothy?

THE DOXOLOGY

"The kingdom of the world has become the kingdom of our Lord and of his Christ." (11:15)

The final section of the Lord's Prayer—"For thine is the kingdom, and the power, and the glory, forever. Amen"—is a doxology so beautiful that it somehow seems almost irreverent to try to dissect it. Some believe that Jesus did not actually say these words. They claim that they were added by someone else at a later date, which is why they are not included in some versions of the Bible. Some manuscripts have it, and some do not. I have looked long at the evidence for and against their inclusion in the sacred Scriptures, and I am perfectly satisfied myself that they were part of Jesus' original pattern of prayer.

The prayer ends as it begins, with an assertion of God's majesty and glory: "Thine is the kingdom." I believe that the emphasis here should be placed on the word "is," to read, "Thine *is* the kingdom"—now.

Despite all appearances to the contrary, God has never abdicated His position as ruler of the universe. What a heartening thought this can be in these days, a thought to fill the soul with song and flood the heart with hope and gladness. It is true that there are many things in the world that militate against His authority—war, poverty, unemployment, drink, gambling, social impurity, and so on. All these seem a flat and final refutation of the phrase "Thine is the kingdom," but their days are numbered. The hour will come when the kingdoms of this world will signal their final surrender and pledge allegiance to their rightful Lord.

PRAYER

O Father, help me to see, despite all the situations and circumstances which might deny Your eternal Kingship, that You are reigning over the world now. Yours is the final control. I am so thankful. Amen.

FURTHER STUDY

Matt. 4:1-11; Obad. 21; Heb. 12:28; 2 Pet. 1:11
Why was Satan's temptation foolish?
How did Jesus respond?

THEIR DAYS ARE NUMBERED

FOR READING AND MEDITATION—
2 THESSALONIANS 2:1-12

"The lawless one will be revealed, whom the Lord Jesus will . . . destroy by the splendour of his coming." (2:8)

Despite all evidences to the contrary, God is in charge of the world's affairs, and the days of rebellious kingdoms on earth are numbered. Our God reigns! The "power and the glory" spoken of in the final words of the Lord's Prayer are talking about kingdom power and glory. The other type of power and glory, that which is measured by earthly standards alone and rejected by Jesus in His temptation in the wilderness, is doomed to dissolution and decay.

Ezekiel the prophet, speaking centuries ago of the impermanence of anything not founded on kingdom values, said, "Your doom appears; your sin has blossomed, your pride has budded" (Ezek. 7:10, Moffatt). Note the telltale steps: doom appears, sin blossoms, and pride has budded. And the fruit of all this? Dissolution and decay.

I have spoken before of my fondness for Moffatt's translation, despite his astonishing liberties with some texts, but I know of nothing that excites me any more than his translation of 2 Thessalonians 2:3. When speaking of a prominent figure who will arise in the last days and challenge the authority of God's kingdom, he refers to him as "the Lawless One, the doomed One." Those who break the laws of God's kingdom, which are written into the very nature of things, are doomed. Perhaps not today, nor tomorrow, but inevitably, anything that is against God's kingdom is destined to destruction. It carries within itself the seeds of its own dissolution and decay.

PRAYER

Gracious Father, I have looked upon the kingdom of the world until my eyes are tired—tired of looking at death. Now lift up my eyes, and let me look at life. Let me look upon You. And I see You, not as a reclining God, but a reigning God. Hallelujah!

FURTHER STUDY

Eph. 6:10-18; John 12:30-31; Heb. 2:14; 1 John 3:8
What is Paul's exhortation?
How can we take dominion?

HE REIGNS—NOW

"To him be the glory forever! Amen." (11:36)

We are seeing that the final part of the Lord's Prayer, which is really a doxology, contains a categorical assertion that God reigns through His kingdom—now. It manifestly requires a measure of faith and courage to affirm this truth in our modern society, when so many things seem positively to shout against it—so many wrongs that clamor for redress, so many problems that demand a solution, and so many social evils whose existence appears utterly incompatible with the reign of God. Yet affirm it we must.

A dear Christian, in a letter to me some time ago, said, "I look around the world and am appalled. My only comfort is the hymn 'Jesus Shall Reign Where'er the Sun.' I, therefore, sit back and watch and wait the day." I told her that her letter reminded me of some words I heard someone put together in a conference once:

> *Sit down, O men of God!*
> *His kingdom He will bring.*

Whenever it shall please His will.
You need not do a thing!

In my reply I said, "Yes, it's true that one day the kingdom of God shall 'stretch from shore to shore,' but let us not ignore the fact that God is reigning now. Given our cooperation, the Almighty can greatly affect the world through our committed lives. If we fail to see this, then it is possible that we struggle and stumble through life, waiting for Him, while all the time He is waiting for us."

PRAYER

O God, deliver me from a view of life that says, "Look what the world is coming to." Help me to look at You; then I can say: "Look what has come to the world." Thank You, Father. Amen.

FURTHER STUDY

Rev. 7:9–17; Exod. 24:17; 40:34; Ps. 19:1; John 1:14
How can we behold His glory?
How is our vision of God enlarged?

"RISE UP, O MEN OF GOD"

FOR READING AND MEDITATION—
PSALM 93:1-5

"The LORD reigns." (93:1)

Although the fullness of God's kingdom is yet to come, there is a sense in which the King is reigning now, and we can say with the utmost certainty, "Our God reigns!"

Previously I mentioned a lady who had written to me, indicating her intention to withdraw from life and await the day when God would finally establish His kingdom in power and glory on the earth. I replied with a parody of a hymn that apparently got her thinking. She wrote back in a few weeks and said, "You were right. I was waiting for God, but now I realize He is waiting for me." She ended her letter with the words of the hymn:

> *Rise up, O men of God!*
> *Have done with lesser tings;*
> *Give heart and soul and mind and strength*
> *To serve the King of kings.*

This, not the parody I referred to in an earlier reading, must indicate our line of action. Yes, of course, the final ushering in of God's kingdom is yet to take place, but that does not mean that He is taking a back seat in the world's affairs. God wants to reign through us!

We need not wait for the day when spectacularly the great God of the universe demonstrates His imperial power. As He sounds forth a rallying cry, even through these pages, respond to Him, I urge you, with a fresh consecration of purpose, and dedicate yourself to letting Him reign through you.

PRAYER

God, I give myself wholly to You, not only just to live in me, but to reign through me. I gladly submit my whole being to You today. Live and reign in me. For Jesus' sake. Amen.

FURTHER STUDY

Rom. 13:1-14; 2 Cor. 10:4; 1 Tim. 1:18; 6:12; 2 Tim. 2:4

How can we overcome the works of darkness?

What was Paul's exhortation to Timothy?

WE GIVE, HE GIVES

FOR READING AND MEDITATION—
EPHESIANS 4:17-32

"Put on the new self, created to be like God." (4:24)

We have now examined, phrase by phrase, the matchless words of the Lord's Prayer. To be effective, prayer must flow out of a truly committed heart. It must be the definition of our spirit, our attitude to God.

An unknown author put it this way:

"I cannot say 'our' if I live only for myself. I cannot say 'Father' if I do not try to act like His child. I cannot say 'who art in heaven' if I am laying up no treasure there.

"I cannot say "hallowed be thy name' if I am not striving for holiness. I cannot say 'thy kindgom come' if I am not doing all in my power to hasten that event.

"I cannot say 'give us this day our daily bread' if I am dishonest or seeking something for nothing. I cannot say 'forgive us our trespasses' if I bear a grudge against another.

"I cannot say 'lead us not into temptation' if I deliberately place myself in its path. I cannot say 'deliver us from evil' if I do not put on the armor of God.

"I cannot say 'thine is the kingdom and the power and the glory' if I do not give the King the loyalty due to Him from a faithful subject.

"And finally, I cannot say 'forever' if the horizon of my life is bounded completely by time."

The whole thrust of the Lord's Prayer is that when we give God His rightful place, He gives us our rightful place.

But not before.

PRAYER

Father, thank You for sharing with me the insights of this prayer.
May I bring my praying more in line with Your praying.
For Jesus' sake. Amen!

FURTHER STUDY

Mark 6:45-56; 1:35; Luke 11:1; 5:16; 6:12
What was the pattern of Christ's life?
What was the disciples' request? Make it yours today.

OTHER BOOKS IN THIS SERIES

If you've enjoyed your experience with this devotional book, look for more Every Day with Jesus® titles by Selwyn Hughes.

Every Day with Jesus: The Lord's Prayer
0-8054-2735-X

Every Day with Jesus: The Spirit-Filled Life
0-8054-2736-8

Available January 2004
Every Day with Jesus: The Character of God
0-8054-2737-6

Available January 2004
Every Day with Jesus: Hinds' Feet, High Places
0-8054-3088-I

Available July 2004
Every Day with Jesus: The Armor of God
0-8054-3079-2

Available July 2004
Every Day with Jesus: Staying Spiritually Fresh
0-8054-3080-6

ALSO BY SELWYN HUGHES

Every Day Light *with paintings by Thomas Kinkade*	0-8054-0188-1
Every Day Light: Water for the Soul *with paintings by Thomas Kinkade*	0-8054-1774-5
Every Day Light: Light for the Path *with paintings by Larry Dyke*	0-8054-2143-2
Every Day Light: Treasure for the Heart *with paintings by Larry Dyke*	0-8054-2428-8
Every Day Light Devotional Journal	0-8054-3309-0
Christ Empowered Living	0-8054-2450-4
Cover to Cover *A Chronological Plan to Read the Bible in One Year*	0-8054-2144-0
Hope Eternal	0-8054-1767-2
Jesus–The Light of the World *with paintings by Larry Dyke*	0-8054-2089-4

The Selwyn Hughes Signature Series

Born to Praise	0-8054-2091-6
Discovering Life's Greatest Purpose	0-8054-2323-0
God: The Enough	0-8054-2372-9
Prayer: The Greatest Power	0-8054-2349-4

Trusted
All Over the World

Daily Devotionals

    Books and Videos

Day and Residential Courses

    Counselling Training

Biblical Study Courses

    Regional Seminars

Ministry to Women

CWR have been providing training and resources for Christians since the 1960s. Fr our headquarters at Waverley Abbey Hous have been serving God's people with a visi help apply God's Word to everyday life an relationships. The daily devotional *Every I with Jesus* is read by over three-quarters of million people in more than 150 countries and our unique courses in biblical studies pastoral care are respected all over the wor

For a free brochure about our seminars and cc or a catalogue of CWR resources please conta at the following address:

CWR,
Waverley Abbey House,
Waverley Lane,
Farnham,
Surrey GU9 8EP

Telephone: 01252 784700
Email: mail@cwr.org.uk
Website: www.cwr.org.uk

CWR CRUSADE FOR WORLD REVIVAL *Applying God's Word to everyday life and rel*